# IF YOU CAN TALK WITH YOUR MOUTH

Unlocking the Extraordinary Power of Your Voice

## Chris Leo

CONTENTS

# INTRODUCTION

There is a reason for every action. There is a purpose for everything. Every part of your body has its function. Your brain is to think and process information. Your eye is to capture images, send them to your brain to process and produce meaningful information. The same with your hands – designed to pick up things. Every part of your body has meaningful assignment in your life. Even the eyebrow that most people shave off has its significance to your being. However, one part of your body decides many outcomes in your life. That part is your mouth.

Your mouth is the gateway to your body. It is the most essential body part for enhancing your life. The progression of human life is directly proportional to the use of mouth. Whether it is fruitfulness, reproduction, sound sleep, academic success, marital success, career success, spiritual welfare and mental health, your mouth decides them all. It sets you free from illnesses and attracts enjoyment in your old age.

The mouth is one part of your body that holds the key to achieving success or failure. We describe the mouth as the door that opens into the world of your whole body. It influences your bodily and emotional well-being in numerous ways.

Regrettably, most of us do not care much about what comes out of our mouths or what goes into it. There is a huge misappropriation of our mouths in our daily living. This is why I am writing this book to show you the potentials that abound in your mouth and how you can harness them for your all-round well-being.

This book explains the great potentials of the mouth from the time of creation. It shows how you can use it to create health, wealth, peace, prosperity, and all manner of blessings. The same mouth can also lead to deficiency, darkness, and death. Whatever it is or would be, is entirely the way you use it. There are no shortcuts, no dodging the protocol. Whatever you wish to see in life depends on what you say with your mouth. That is why you should read this book.

If you are someone who is rigid in thinking, you may encounter a challenge reading this book. This is because some of the issues raised here are not conventional and may appear illogical. If you are a seeker of reason in every deal, then you may find it hard believing. Nevertheless, if you wish to engage in a reading experiences that can change your life, then read this book with an open mind to the last page. You will surely learn one or more things that will add value to your life.

I have used rich texts from history to explain why you should take care of your mouth. You will also find examples of men and women who used their mouths either the wrong way or the right way, and what they attracted to themselves. This book is rich in powerful content that will open your eyes to some things you never knew about the potentials of your mouth. As you discover them in this book and begin to harness them, you will find that what your mouth cannot do does not really exist anywhere in the world. Enjoy the read!

*Chris Leo*

6

<u>CHAPTER ONE</u>

MOUTH: CONDUIT TO CREATION

In the beginning, God created the heaven and the earth. This is the first line you will read in the Holy bible. What follows is the description of the earth – it was empty and shapeless. The question is: How did God create the heaven and the earth? What follows the description of earth may be the clue. Let me bullet the few features of the earth at this point:

a.    The earth was shapeless. That is, it was without a definite desirable form. What the Creator was seeing was not what He wanted to see.

b.    The earth was empty. History captures it as an empty waste. You cannot have an empty house and you call it a home.

c.    The earth was full of darkness. That is to say, that darkness covered the entire earth space. No part of it had light. Now, you cannot enjoy living in a house without light. No matter what you fill it with, you will not be happy to live in it without seeing what is in it when you want to see them.

d.      The waters cover the earth. There was no land so how could you possibly like that. If your house were on a lake, you would still need an access road on the land to use. Even if you are to build a bridge, the bridge cannot start on water and end on the water. There has to be some piece of dry land.

Now these four features describe what the first creation of God was like. Some other history translators used the word 'chaotic' to add to its description of being shapeless. There was no orderliness, no beauty in the arrangement and sure no special designs that can attract your fancy. However, the Creator needed to make it appear better, more organized, desirable and beautiful to behold. So he did something – He used his mouth.

History said, *'And God said, Let there be light, and there was light'*. That is what changed the whole picture. It changed the entire outlook of the earth. The darkness disappeared. The picture came out clearer. One could see the rest of the elements of nature. You can now think of the next action or phase of the plan to take on. With the presence of the light, you can focus on areas you want to start and develop according to your plan. Now that was for the earth.

All through that historical phase, our Creator used His mouth. When He saw that light has appeared and it was good, He endorsed it because it was pleasant and suitable for the next thing He wanted to do. He proceeded to the next phase. He separated the light He made with his mouth from the darkness that He met on ground. It did not end there; He used His mouth again to name the light 'Day' and called the darkness 'Night'. In essence, the Day and Night we have today are results of the use of the mouth. They did not just happen on their own.

Therefore, if you go through the history lines as recorded in the Holy Bible, you will see God using His mouth to call things into existence. Not only that, he used His mouth to change their form and shapes to what he wanted them to look like. As he was speaking and calling forth things into existence, he was also giving them the names that he believed suited them. Obviously, this was all he did all through the six days he created the earth before he took a break for just one day.

How does this relate to your life? When you look into your life, you might see some similarities with the shapeless, empty earth space full of darkness. If you look critically at some areas of your life, it might shock you, that is, if you did not know it before now, to find some dark spots that you desire could be lighted up.

No one is perfect in every area of their lives, so you need to check those areas that need recreation. You know what, your Creator empowered you to be like him, think like him and do as he did. He was not comfortable with the environment of the earth that He formed in the beginning so He decided to employ His mouth to recreate things. He used that part of Him that He also gave you for that purpose. Your mouth is the transformer of your old world into a new world.

The reason you are not having a new lease on life is that you have neglected the transformer you were given at creation. The reason it appears your life is filled with confusion is that you have not called forth the light domiciled in you. You are complaining of a formless and messy life because you are yet to employ the services of the tool for the reconfiguration of your entire being. If only you could recognize the tool He gave you and use it as He did with His, no area of your life will harbor any shadow let alone darkness.

How to Use Your Mouth Effectively

The fact that your mouth is the transformer of your life is not enough to achieve a new you. You can use it in many ways to achieve a new world you desire. It is also true that you could use it and yet not achieve much that you seek. This is why I am going to highlight few ways you can use your mouth effectively to arrive at the new atmosphere that will gladden your heart. You need to know these few ways because they will help you to relate to other issues relating to your mouth as discussed in the remaining chapters of this book.

Your Mouth Should Speak Faith

If you must talk, please talk faith. Before you engage your mouth, first engage your heart. That is where the transformation begins. With your heart, you must believe what you wish to say with your mouth. There must be a conviction that what you want to say is what you wish to see. More important, you must believe that it has already been settled in your heart by faith. Do not walk by sight but by faith. Your faith will always conquer what your fears cannot overcome.

You do not really need to have perfect conditions before you say something that you want to see in your life. You just have to see it with the eyes of faith, trusting that they will happen as you envision them. All you need is a strong conviction of the possibility of that thing happening. Since there is a potential in it, do not allow logic to stop you from trying to harness it. Once your heart is convinced, your mouth can confess. Declaration comes after decision. It's the way your heart and mouth cooperate to recreate and reconfigure your world.

## Your Mouth Should Agree With Your Heart

If your mouth is saying something different from what your heart is engaging, there will be no effectiveness. No result will come out of the exercise.

There must be an agreement between your heart and your mouth. Remember these are two different parts or organs of your body. They have different functions but are tightly connected to work for your well-being. This is why you must ensure that your heart is not far from your mouth and vice versa. Your heart decides while your mouth declares the decision. Your heart molds the idea while your mouth molds the reality.

Therefore, before you open your mouth, you must open the depths of your heart to see clearly, what has been molded inside. This exercise is essential for the realization of the result you wish to see in your life. The coordination must be done properly in order for the manifestation to be well pronounced and obvious. Even in medical science, your mouth is connected to your heart. And the Lord himself corroborated this by saying, *'Out of the abundance of the heart, the mouth speaks'*.

Your mouth is the channel through which the contents of your heart flows out. It's like an outlet; a pipe that lets water out from the source. Your mouth does not really produce the words, your heart does. So what your mouth does is to agree with your heart's decision and instruction to speak out what has been decided. But you have to train your mouth to speak exactly what your heart decides. The same way, train or exercise your heart to mold the right things your mouth should say.

Your Mouth Must Speak Right

Right words produce right ways. Right words give light and direction even to the lost. When God spoke the right words to the empty, chaotic mass of darkness at the beginning of creation, what came out of it was light. Right words are the seeds that are sown into every situation to produce a different set of right conditions. Most people do not know how to direct their mouths to say the right things that can help their conditions. Instead they let their words come out unguarded and misguided, and this causes harm to them or to those who hear them.

The Ephesians had a problem with this so Apostle Paul wrote to them about the right use of their mouths. He said, *'Let no corrupt communication proceed out of your mouth, but that which is good to the use of edifying, that it may minister grace unto the hearers'*. People around you want to hear words that can help their condition not worsen it. You may not even know this: Your ears love to hear right words. So each time you say the wrong things, your ears grow weak. As there's connection between your mouth and your heart, so there's a connection between your ears and your mouth.

The interconnectivity of your body parts requires you to learn how to use them to enhance the proper functioning of one another. Anything you say affects the others in ways that you can never imagine — positively or negatively. Your mouth is a sower of seeds. Just like your hands, you control the direction to do something you wish to do. So learn to say the right words at all times. This is the only guaranty for the right results you wish to see and enjoy.

To help your mouth to speak right always, use it wisely. It is not compulsory that you say everything you feel like saying. You must learn restraint sometimes. This is because what you say cannot be retracted even if you say, Sorry, I withdraw my earlier statement. For example, if you use your mouth to say some hurtful things about someone, the person is already hurt. Coming back few minutes later to say that you are sorry does not really take away the person's hurts. You have just spoiled their day and joy with your mouth. So you should watch what your mouth says. This will lead us to another point.

## Guard Your Mouth with Wisdom

The wisest president that ever lived cautioned his listeners to guard their heart with all diligence. This is because out of the heart are the issues or springs of life. Now you should learn something from it. Guard your mouth with all wisdom too. No matter how good a talker you are, there are places you do not go talking anyhow or saying anything as you wish. Most people who are careless with their mouths have said some things that put them into trouble. Listen to this wise counsel from the wisest king:

*'Be not forward (self-assertive and boastfully ambitious) in the presence of the king, and stand not in the place of great men; for better it is that it should be said to you, Come up here, than that you should be put lower in the presence of the prince, whose eyes have seen you. Rush not forth soon to quarrel [before magistrates or elsewhere], lest you know not what to do in the end when your neighbor has put you to shame. Argue your cause with your neighbor himself; discover not and disclose not another's secret. Lest he who hears you revile you and bring shame upon you and your ill repute have no end. A word fitly spoken and in*

*due season is like apples of gold in settings of silver.'*

Everything he said from the first line was summarized in the last line: *'A word fitly spoken and in due season is like apples of gold in settings of silver.'* That is to say, you should not be forward with your mouth; learn to apply restrain over it. No matter how much you have in your heart to say, be wise to wait until you are given the opportunity to say it. This does not mean you should shut your mouth from speaking, rather it talks about when you are in the company of others. More importantly when you are in the presence of great, influential people.

The next time you want to say something, pause and ponder over it. As you engage your heart also bridle your tongue. Your mouth can rule your world as well as ruin it. It depends how you use it. President Solomon said again, *'He who guards his mouth keeps his life, but he who opens wide his lips comes to ruin.'* What this means is that if you open your mouth to say anyhow words, ruins await.

It is then wise that you apply wisdom before you open your mouth to speak. You shouldn't let your words put you to shame as President Solomon noted would be the result of careless and unguarded talk. You want to enjoy the fruits of your lips, not to endure them. Then, watch it before you say it.

CHAPTER TWO

DOOR TO DEATH AND LIFE

Life is in words. So also is death in what we say. The power to create both lies in our mouth. Those who speak life usually see life and more life. But those who speak death do not live long enough to share their story. With their mouths, they cut short their lives, and leave their families mourning their painful deaths. In this chapter, we shall see how we can create life or cause death with our mouth. The proverbs of Solomon says, *'Death and life are in the power of the tongue, and they who indulge in it shall eat the fruit of it [or death or life].'* I bet you love life, not death.

Words Can Kill

Eugene Peterson translates those proverbs of Solomon in these lines: *'Words kill, words give life; they're either poison or fruit —you choose'*. What this means is that words from your mouth can either kill or keep lives safe. You may wonder how you can kill with your mouth. Perhaps, all you know is that people are killed with guns, clubs, machetes, and any other objects. You sure do know that people are killed by being injected with poisoned substances. Probably you have not seen just one person who died by the mouth of someone else. No worries, you will see it from available and authentic history records.

The first approach to giving an answer is by defining the word, 'kill'. The most authentic book to get this from is the dictionary. I suppose you have one around you or on your smart phone. To kill means to put to death; to extinguish the life of something. It means to render inoperative; to stop, cease, or render void. It is to incapacitate; to produce feelings of revulsion and dissatisfaction. To kill also means to overpower, overwhelm, or defeat something or someone. Another look at it shows that it is to force a company out of business or liquidate a firm.

The above are just some of the meanings of 'kill', which apply to our discussion. So you see that killing does not only happen when you shoot with a gun or cut with a machete or even hit with a stick. You can kill with your mouth. This kind of death is the most painful and most terrifying form of death. Most people would choose to die of gunshots or sword slash rather than by the words of their enemies. Words may not kill instantly as gunshots do, but the slow kind of death is what makes it most dangerous and undesirable.

When Solomon said that words kill, he was talking about rendering someone or something 'inoperative'. Many centuries later, Jesus Christ came on the scene and echoed the same thing in another perspective. *'But I tell you, on the day of judgment men will have to give account of every idle (inoperative, nonworking) word they speak.'* This was recorded by the Tax-collector-turned-disciple, Matthew in his book. Why would God judge every idle or inoperative word? It is because they are out of order. They do not yield positive result. It's same with words that render lives and businesses useless on earth. They put people out of existence and businesses out of operation.

How You Kill with Words

1.     By placing a curse on someone. This is one way most people render others void and vain. A curse is a word that is used to cause supernatural detriment or hindrance to someone. To curse is to use offensive or morally inappropriate language on someone. Such words can devastate the person, and throw them into a state of depression that can

lead to their physical death. When you place a curse on someone, you practically place them in the arms of depression and the cold hands of death. You may not know this, but that's what happens when you use your mouth wrongly to curse and not to bless.

2.     By slandering someone. Gossip may be sweet when you are doing it, but the fruit of it is usually bitter in the end. When you speak evil of another or share false information about them, you kill their image or personality. To slander means to maliciously speak or publish a false statement that is injurious to someone's reputation. It means to defame someone with the intention of reducing or rubbishing their worth. And when that action works as intended, the person could develop heart attack and consequently die. No one else would be held responsible but you.

3.     By mocking someone. For young people in particular, this is serious. Your mouth is not for making mockery of others you feel are not as nice or jolly as you wish. You do not change people or win their association by bullying them. When you bully someone, you

are actually injuring their heart, and it can lead them into worrying about it until they become 'dead' inside. Most children die of traumatic attacks from bullying. They do not have the absorber for the shock it causes them especially if what you say about them is true.

Some people could be poor or suffering some form of sickness, you should not use their condition to mock them. Mocking them is making them feel worthless and no one likes that feeling. It harms their esteem and extinguish their spirit. You have no right whatsoever to take their lives from them with words from your mouth.

Let me leave you with some lines of the lyrics of the song, 'I Need You' by Hezekiah Walker and the Love Fellowship Choir:

I won't hurt you with words from my mouth

I love you, I need you to survive.

My emphasis is on 'I won't hurt you with words from my mouth'. When you hurt people by placing a curse on them; slandering them; mocking them –

you are killing them gradually with your mouth. And I'm sure you wouldn't want to be a murderer. So stop killing with words, and start giving life with your words.

Words Give Life

When was the last time you say something beautiful to yourself? What was it you can recall that you said to someone and they smiled back at you? We are filled with upsetting memories of our ordeals with living life that we often forget to complement ourselves. Life could be so hard on you to the extent that you do not see the need to tell yourself, 'I love me'. Self-love is no longer a virtue for so many people. They condemn themselves before they even get a chance to defend themselves. That style of living does not produce anything better than death. But you can reverse it with your mouth beginning from now.

Death is a function of both words and actions, so also is life. If God could change the atmosphere from the beginning of creation with His words, you can do the same. I do not want to bring in the episodes where Christ gave people life even when they were dead. You may say that is God, and you are not God. Sure, you are not God, neither am I, but we are gods. Both King David and Jesus Christ told us that we are gods. So you can make dead things to come to life again. You can turn around a dead fortune and make it successful. You must have heard of people who resuscitated dying businesses and they became highly flourishing. That is what we are talking about. And certainly, they are not God.

How Your Words Can Give Life

1.      Speak words of faith and hope. I did say that words are seeds sown in the heart of people or in your own heart. To give life by speaking words of faith implies that you say things that boost someone's trust and confidence. Sometimes, your faith plummets. You come face to face with situations that challenge your trust in God and confidence in your abilities. At that moment you are tempted to surrender to the challenge. But the right words from your mouth can push the button up and you overcome.

The same applies to other people. You can give people back their lives by speaking words of faith to them. Most of the people you meet at place of work or other places will encounter moments they want to take their own lives. That should be the right atmosphere to help them live and not die. I read a story, also saw it in a movie. A woman who had lost her loving husband and was left alone in the house wanted to commit suicide few years after. This particular day, she had hung a rope from the ceiling fan and was counting the hours to her death.

Meanwhile, a boy and his father were in the street sharing some gospel tracts. It began to rain so the man told his son they should go home. The little boy insisted of giving out the last copy of the tract in his hand, and that led him to the door of this suicide-bound woman. He knocked heavily until this widow came to door to see who was distracting her from her intended mission to end her life. Behold, it was a little boy wet in the rain and full of smiles. 'Hello ma'am. Just wanna give you this. God loves you'.

The woman reluctantly took the piece of paper not so sure of the words she heard from the mouth of the boy. As she got inside, her hands trembling and heart racing through those words: 'God loves you'. She could feel hope returning, and those words echoing in her heart. In tears she prayed and that canceled the death that was just waiting to take her away. The words of those little boy restored faith and hope that all would be well again. Her faith in God came back. Her hope for a happier future filled her heart. She did not die but live. This is one way your words can give life to someone.

2.      **Speak words of healing**. Many hearts are hurting. They are filled with pain instead of praises. They are full of sores instead of songs. There's so much heaviness that erode the emotions that occupies the hearts of so many people. As a result, they are sick in their spirit, soul and body. What they need is healing. This healing is not by medicine or tablets, but the words of your mouth. President Solomon said, *'Pleasant words are as a honeycomb, sweet to the mind and healing to the body'*. So you see that words can heal any wounded heart or sick mind.

Speaking words of healing does not refer to prayers for one's supernatural healing. It's okay to do that, but that is not what I'm talking about. I mean saying words that remove bitterness and relieves someone of pain in their heart. You do not need to be a Christian or a religious person to do this. It's not for priests and pastors only, but for every human being.

Motivational speakers use this art so well in their presentations. When you listen to a good one, you can overcome the sickness of depression and cancel any intention of committing suicide. When this happens, it is simply healing. Emotional healing is the most sought for healing in the world today. Instead of saying what will hurt, you can choose to speak words that heal.

3.	Speak words of encouragement. As I write, someone out there wants to quit a job, a marriage or doing good things for others. If you look around you, there could be someone ready to give up on the legitimate pursuit of their visions. Some want to just close down a business and go home to 'die'. What such people need is your words of encouragement.

Your words can motivate them to push forward. Your words can inspire them to hold on. Your words can keep them back from throwing in the towel. Because when they do these things, their families that depend on them will suffer the dire consequences. If that man closed down that business, it could affect his family and this could lead to untold hardship. Anything can go wrong; some people do not have the balls to survive hardships. But with words from your mouth, they can get some encouragement.

This last statement reminds me of a business colleague of my now aged father. That man had multiple streams of income in the manufacturing industry. At that time, he had three cars and lived in a well-furnished four-bedroom apartment with his wife. They had no child. He was doing well but the challenges of running those businesses were also there. No one could see he had those challenges. All looked okay but indeed not okay.

One Sunday morning, he drove to his office block, climbed over the fence into the compound, went to his headquarters office and hung himself with a rope from the ceiling fan. The guards on duty only discovered few hours after they did not see him come out of the compound. No one foresaw that death coming. The note he left read: 'Let me end it all'. He was simply tired of life. And perhaps, no one was able to speak words to encourage him to hang in there.

Those few words, 'Do not give up!' would have saved his life, but they were not coming from the mouth of anyone around. Be ready to say those words to yourself and to others in need of them. You never know who you might just save if not yourself.

4.    Speak words of restrain. You can actually keep someone from dying not only by speaking words of healing, faith or encouragement. You can deliver people from death by restraining them with your words. 'Do not kill yourself; life is beautiful' is a powerful message that can save so many lives. But how many of us use them to save lives?

Two men were locked up in a prison. At midnight, all they could do was to start singing some hymns. As they were singing, a great earthquake rocked the place and flung the doors of each cell open. The jailer got awake and drew a dagger to kill himself supposing that the inmates had escaped. But one of the two men restrained him by shouting, *'Do not harm yourself, for we are all here!'* That was how Apostle Paul saved the man's life. Even though he was an inmate, he used his mouth to save the jailer. Every life is precious and you can help keep them so with your mouth.

32

# CHAPTER THREE

## HOSEPIPE TO HEALTH

Words give life, they give health too. It is someone who is healthy that can say they are truly alive. Just as you can use your mouth to save the dying and keep them alive, you can use your mouth to keep yourself and others healthy. You can deal with any signs of ill-health in you with words from your mouth.

### Your Mouth Affects Your Health

Since the mouth can create, it can as well destroy. And since it can destroy, it can restore what is destroyed. When a centurion's servant was sick, he came to Christ begging Him to heal the young man. Jesus said, Fine, let's go and I will heal your servant. The centurion objected, No sir, just stand here and speak the word, and my servant will be healed. This man believed in the power of spoken words. He did not see the need for Christ to come lay His hands, since He could say something and it would be done.

Now you may say, that was Christ who could do anything. That's not the point. The man's belief is what I'm pointing out here. He was not a Christian yet he understood the power in the mouth to reverse ill-health and restore the sick person to health. He simply teaches us how to use our mouth to affect our health. But there's another side of it. You can use your mouth also to attract ill-health to yourself. It works in both ways.

Solomon really captured this in his proverbial book when he said, *'The tongue of the wise utters knowledge rightly, but the mouth of the [self-confident] fool pours out folly'*. What is knowledge here? The understanding of facts. There must be strong basis for deciding something is real or not. So your mouth can affect your health in many ways. Let's look at a few of them.

1.    When you do not speak out of accurate knowledge. When you feel you are unwell, what do you say? Remember, it's just a feeling, you are not sure yet. Most people who have a history of a particular illness are the worst affected in this regard. Once that feeling comes, they say, 'Not again; that sickness has come again.' They did not run a medical test to ascertain what it is; they just claim it on

themselves. You are simply not uttering knowledge rightly, according to Solomon.

You feel slight pain in your head, not sure of what it is, and you jump into conclusion that it is headache or migraine. That is uttering or speaking out of insufficient information. The painful part is that, you attract it to yourself by your words.

If you understand the power in your mouth, you will not say something about your health when you are not sure about it. Even if you are familiar with that symptom, you should know that one cannot be too sure of the exact health issue without proper diagnosis. So the wisest thing to do is to go for some medical tests to be sure. Do not claim a disease that is not there because the test result may say something different.

The slight pain in the head may be a result of not getting enough sleep. It's only natural that you feel it. It may also be as a result of much stress. What you need is to get some sleep, some rest, and then watch it again. Most times it goes away. Rest is a powerful analgesic to such pains. Where you do not know this simple but often unknown secret, you use your mouth to declare yourself sick when in essence the symptoms are signs of stress.

There is a connection between words and health. Psychologically, words do more than medicine in some cases. It's been found that just saying the right words to a sick patient gives them relief even before they are given drugs. Imagine then what would happen if these same folks speak to themselves about their feelings. If someone speaks to you and you feel alright, then it is wise you learn to speak wellness into your own body. If you knew that words bring relief, I suppose you wouldn't wait for someone to speak to you; you would speak to yourself based on that knowledge. This is one way you use your mouth to positively affect your health and wellness.

2.     Do not speak out of fear. Fear makes people claim what is not there. The proverbs of Solomon said that a lazy man claims there's a lion on the way. Yet other people take that same road. Careful study has shown that apprehension of death kills people faster than death itself. This is because of the bad news

they hear. And what is bad news? It is a collection of negative words published from sad events. Some people become sick immediately this negative information filters into their ears. They begin to utter words that imply they would be seriously affected, too.

There is a measure of fear that is alright which indicates that you are not a robot. As long as you wear flesh and blood flows through it, you have this measure of natural fear. But there's another dimension that is not healthy. When you begin to entertain fear of the unknown due to the bad news you hear daily, you are going to be sick. If you then begin to make some confessions, utter some words in agreement with that news, it begins to affect your health badly.

For example, you hear that there is outbreak of measles in town, and immediately you begin to say, Oh no, it's going to get to my children. Watch it: it might get to them. You have used your mouth to attract the measles to your household even when the disease is far away from them. This is not a Christian or religious thing; it's spiritual, depending on your knowledge of what is spiritual. I'm not trying to sound religious here because this book is not about religion; it's about the real life. The truth is: the real life is spiritual.

Your words carry such power that can draw things to you. That's why they are seeds. You sow them anyhow, you have anyhow fruits. In practical sowing, you are careful what and how you sow. You are intentional about it. In the same way, you should be intentional about your words; they should not spew out of your mouth unintentionally. Let me share a personal experience with you. Perhaps it will inspire you to get the point more clearly.

Sometime in November 2018, my youngest child caught chickenpox. You should know that this virus is infectious, that is, it is transmittable. Soon after, it infected my two other children, and few days later, my wife. All four of them were infected and became sick at the same time. I was left to take care of them most of the time. Some people said, Hey man, do this and do that so it doesn't infect you too. They all believed that but I said with my mouth, this thing cannot touch me.

I took care of my children — bath them, attended to them, helped them until they all were well again. Each day, I told my body, listen: you are not for this. You cannot contract this infection. You are too strong to be infected, and so on. Nothing happened to me. I did not respond out of fear that it spread from my 5 year old boy to the two older ones and then to my wife in the same small apartment. I used my mouth to decide what I wanted. If I do not permit it, it will not stay. That's my story. Now, you can make it your story too if you would not respond out of fear the next time you feel or see or hear bad news. You decide what happens.

3.    Speak what you want to see not what you see. Another way you can affect your health with your mouth is never to announce your feelings or imaginations. Instead announce what you want to see about your health. With your mouth you can change the trajectory of your health. You have the power in your mouth to tell your body how it should be. O yes! I told you what I did when that infectious disease struck my family. I did not respond or react out of fear. If I did, no matter what I was saying, it

would have infected me. This is because my heart is not in agreement with my mouth.

Remember at the beginning of this book, I did say that it's important that there's concord between what's in your heart and what you say with your mouth. If the content of our heart and the confession of your mouth are going in parallel directions, you are likely not going to see the result you expect.

So to decide the flow and state of your health, you must begin to see sound health, not sickness. You must envisage yourself living in health and follow up with speaking forth what you see. Speaking forth is so important to achieving the sound health you desire. This is the secret of most people who hardly visit the hospital except for medical checkups. I bet you do not like to be sick. No one really wants to be sick. You desire sound health and it can be yours if you just trust and do exactly what you are reading in this book. I have tried them, and found them the best way to stay healthy and keep fit. The only extra thing is good diet plus physical exercise for physical fitness.

Health is not just feeling feverish or having malaria or arthritis. Someone can be sick in the mind. Some people feel they are going to run mad, die suddenly and experience such horrible things. It comes to them from time to time, and they feel helpless. Anytime they see someone, they complain, 'hey, I feel like going crazy', 'I feel like I'm going to die', or 'I see myself falling ill'. Something is not right with their health system. They need this book to help them save their lives from becoming what they are seeing and saying.

A 20-year old boy was telling his friends that he felt like killing himself. He saw himself killing himself. And couple of weeks later, he drank a bottle of concentrated herbicide and died within hours. With his mouth he said what he was seeing, and he did what he was seeing. He died.

If he knew the power of his mouth and how to use it to upturn what he was seeing, he would be alive. He should be saying, 'No way, I'm not going to die. I cannot kill myself, no, I will not. I've got life to live. I've got friends who love me and family, too. There's a place for me in life. I cannot disappoint all people who believe in me. So that picture of dying or death isn't for me. Now, I will live and not die.' Again, this isn't a religious thing. It's an exercise of the powers invested on you from creation by your Creator, but often neglected out of insufficient knowledge.

There is no doubt you see things that you do not wish to happen in your life. They come as imaginations, and impress themselves so strong on your mind that you are tempted to share them with someone. Before long you begin to feel sick in your body, and it seems what you see is happening already. You can change that immediately. Trust me, you can, with your mouth.

First, be calm and ask yourself, what do I want to see in my life? This picture or that one. Once you settle it, begin to say it with your mouth. You could feel the pressure of saying that strong impression, but since you have resolved what you want to see, go ahead and declare it with your mouth. Do this daily, hourly, every minute if possible. Say it in your bathroom, bedroom, kitchen, anywhere you do not have a crowd so they do not think you are running crazy.

Then, watch that picture of ill-health vanish. And that negative feeling dissipate. And you become strong again in your mind and body. For further help on this, get my books titled, *'Think Ahead, See Ahead'*, *'Power Plugs for Superlative Performance'*, and *'Activating the Power of Your Creative Mind'*.

So dear, you can help yourself keep healthy with your mouth or remain sick with your mouth too. It's all a choice that we all must make. I choose to be healthy. The last time I visited a clinic was three years ago when I had malaria fever. It was due to mosquito bites, which was common in my environment at the time. I check my BP, Sugar level, Blood level, weight, etc. I'm doing just fine.

I'm no super human; I just know the secret. I have the knowledge of what causes the feeling, and how to address it beginning with the confession of my mouth. I rest if it is stress, drink enough water for easy digestion, and do some physical exercise to stay fit. Most importantly, I tell myself with my mouth every

day that I am just fine. That is how you will be if
you do the same.

CHAPTER FOUR

WAY TO WEALTH

The first requirement for wealth is your mind. The second is your mouth. Your mind thinks wealth, your mouth speaks it. They say that if you want to be a millionaire then talk like a millionaire. Those who said so are right. There's a strong connection between your mouth and your money. This is what I want us to look at in this chapter. How you can bring your wealth closer to you with your mouth and your confessions. As I have maintained, you do not have to be religious to make this happen; it's about your psyche, too. So, let's see how to make this happen.

Speak Prosperity, Not Poverty

A particular civil servant-turned preacher was reading a book and suddenly came to a point that he rushed outside and shouted, 'I cannot be poor!' Those who heard him thought he had gone mad that afternoon. Today, he is the richest preacher in that country and one of the 10 richest preachers in the world. His mouth gave him his money!

Your mouth is another way to decide your wealth. When you are working hard, what do you say about what you expect? I guess you would say, I am going to be rich and successful. That sounds like what every other person would say, but that's not the case. Some people would still say they are not sure of what would happen though they are working hard. That's the difference between the rich and the poor. What they see and what they say.

To speak prosperity does not mean there's no possibility of failure. Failure is always a possibility as success is. But you must choose either and declare it with your mouth. Like in creating life and attracting sound health, the approach is the same. You can speak things into existence. It does not mean you do not work hard or think smart, but if you do all these and still say the opposite, I bet you will achieve nothing. A man can hardly succeed beyond what he sees and speaks. This is why you must learn to use your mouth well as you use your mind or brain.

Solomon said in one of many proverbs, *'Will you set your eyes upon wealth, when [suddenly] it is gone? For riches certainly make themselves*

*wings, like an eagle that flies toward the heavens'.*
This wise president of ancient Israel was talking about being filled with desperation for riches. He was not condemning having riches but was cautioning against the danger of trying to get rich at all cost.

In the process he made a remarkable revelation about the nature of wealth. Riches have wings and can fly. Wow! You see that! So if wealth can fly away, figuratively speaking, they can fly in, too. That's wonderful to know. That means they behave like animated things. They can take form. Someone said that until you build home for wealth it won't come in. This is agreeing with what Solomon said about wealth having wings. This means you invite it with your mouth while working with your mind and hands.

Now, what that suggests is that you can speak prosperity into your life as well as speak poverty into your life. It is all in your mouth. While you are working, you are talking. While you are smarting it out in your work, you are also speaking it out to work. You keep saying it; keep telling yourself and anyone who cares to listen that you're going to make it. Wealth can come by words! I can tell you this confidently from personal experience. Listen to wealthy people, they knew they were going to be rich. They did not bump into wealth by chance. Yes, they worked hard but they used their words to shape the result.

After all, some people work harder but never become rich. Most of them end in poverty or low life because they speak little of their expectation. This is out of fear they may be mocked if what they say do not happen – who cares! Your duty is to say it, whether it works or not should not bother you. Guess what, it works! That preacher was mocked for years after he began to speak out everywhere that he would never be poor. But one day, his audacious confessions came true. Today, his major message is on faith; that if you see it, believe it and say it, it will work. You cannot take that away from him, and his followers are becoming rich by that same principle. You should make it your principle too and see success come embracing you.

There is one good thing this speaking forth will do for you. It will keep you conscious of what you are expecting. It makes your pursuit more definite. Once you are saying it, you wouldn't want to slack your hands, instead you work more towards achieving it. You can hardly give up when you are always telling yourself that you will be rich. As you say it every time, your spirit stays alert, your mind stays receptive to ideas, and you are always ready to clinch opportunities to make it happen. So what is there to lose? I bet, nothing.

See Possibility, Not Impossibility

While you are at it speaking forth and calling your harvest into existence, be sure you are working. You cannot be idle and lazy and expect someone else's harvest to fly into your store. It does not happen. As you labor, you also speak favor to your labor. However, there's a challenge to this. The questions will come to your mind time and again: Is this possible? Am I not really going nuts? How can someone possibly attract wealth by just speaking? Yeah, they say, if you want to be like a billionaire, talk and act like one. Isn't that insane? Lots of questions in your mind can make you doubt the possibility. But it is possible.

Possibility and impossibility exist in your mind. Every rich business man that sees opportunity to make good money, sees the possibility. There are always odds; there are probabilities. But they concentrate more on the pluses. What you hear them say is, 'I'm going to make lots of money. This deal looks great; it's going to fetch me good money'. That is seeing possibility. If you are a pessimist, you will hardly be rich. This is because you often doubt the possibility of something happening. It doesn't make sense to you if you cannot perfectly put the pieces together.

Take the current world's richest man as example. If Elon Musk had not seen the possibility of buying Twitter, he wouldn't go for it. He must have sat himself down and said, 'Hey, I am going to get this company. I will be the new CEO in months to come'. And as the months went by and the weeks drew near, he kept telling himself that. Then he made the move. While telling yourself that you are going to succeed and become rich, you have to see the picture and possibility of it coming through. The only thing that is impossible is what you see and say is impossible. This is however to be put into proper context. And that will be our next point.

Speak What Is Possible

There are levels of prosperity.  Wealth comes in stages too. Even though it is good to see possibilities in everything you do, yet you must understand there are levels of attainment in life.

Let's use Elon Musk as example again. Before he bought Twitter, he was part of the corporation. He was a shareholder in the company. Besides, he had the financial and technological structures to buy it. Let's say he did not know anything about it and did not have the structures to even bid for it, he would end at seeing it as a possibility, which is like dreaming about it. He may not be able to succeed because it's beyond him. So while dreaming and seeing possibilities, speak the prosperity that is truly possible.

You have read about Solomon the wisest and richest president and commander in chief that ever lived. He was so rich that no leader before him or after him got to his level. But you have to understand that he did not ask for it; God decided to give it to him. We can say that his wealth was a result of God's spectacular and sovereign act.

There are acts like that we can readily see in history. They are not something you begin to ask or speak to happen because they were done to show the sovereignty of the Almighty God. So such is not the kind of wealth you speak into happening no matter the faith in your heart. Otherwise, you injure your heart and bruise your mind expecting it to happen.

So, in speaking prosperity and seeing possibilities, speak the possibility that is really possible. You can create wealth by making powerful utterances over your work and labor. Making wishes is not what we are talking about. Wishes are mere speculations without a substantial backing. You cannot speak money out of the woods. You look at what you have and speak to have it increased. Even Christ the miracle worker did not feed the multitude from the sand. He could do that, but that would be leaving us with the option of laziness. Someone provided the bread and the fish, then He multiplied them by speaking forth with His mouth. This is the right way, embrace it and do the same.

<u>CHAPTER FIVE</u>

CHALLENGES TO EFFECTIVE USE OF YOUR MOUTH

It has been said that to enjoy longevity, you need to eat healthy diets and add daily physical exercise to it. These are good but you need to do this too: Use your mouth daily by speaking the right words. This has the potential of adding more days to you than food and physical exercise. Your words are power plugs to fire you into your new levels each day. However there are challenges that come with using our mouths effectively. In concluding this book, let us look at some of them. Whether in recreating your world or bringing wealth and health, these challenges show up at every stage of our lives.

Compromising Your Belief System

Belief system is a powerful stronghold on people of different backgrounds. While some people are religious, others are irreligious. While some believe in deities, others do not believe in them. Some believe in faith, others believe in facts. All these beliefs pose a serious challenge to understanding the points made in this book. But whether you believe in God or not, in faith or not, there is one thing that stands out, and that is the result you will get when you apply the truths unveiled in this book.

Where there is result, what you believe in rarely counts. The man who believes in getting well by the administration of drugs is not different from the man who believes in faith to get well. The only difference is that the former spends his money buying the drugs while the other expends his faith and no money. Which would you rather choose? The latter, I guess. Yet there's a challenge to making this choice. It's all in avoiding to compromise what you believe.

Compromise is about give and take. It does not mean that what you believe in is no longer authentic, rather, that you decide to try something else that is working. As long as it does not take away your peace and sleep, there's no harm in trying it. But if you are someone who has a strong belief in drugs to get well, you will find it hard to practice faith. If you are also someone who strongly believes in hard work only as a way to become wealthy, this book will challenge that belief. Remember, no one says that you should not work hard; in fact, you have to. But something else helps it, your confession that your hard work will pay off. This sounds spiritual, right? Now let me come in with that.

The entire world is immersed in a spiritual atmosphere, and you must come to understand that. Everything you see is being controlled by what you do not see. This is not about religion but reality. Actions do not just happen. Science doesn't just emerge from the blues. There are forces at play in the world both good and bad forces. The actions or happenings you see are being controlled or brought into effect by words.

These words are spoken by voices you do not hear unless you are connected to the supernatural realm. The sounds of thunder and lightning are all voices uttered in that realm. There are spirits that live and move freely among us you cannot see with your optical eyes. The only thing that helps mortals to see and understand these things is faith. You just believe and it happens.

It is by this faith that someone can actually agree to find a middle ground with another person's idea. It is this faith that will make both the religious and irreligious to accept some principles that are not common to them, neither harmful to their beliefs. Yet faith still remains a big challenge to all despite the fact that it does not take away their sleep or peace.

But for those who decide to open up to faith, they always find themselves triumphing over all odds. The good life is achieved when you decide to have an open mind and a flexible will. It makes you want to concede in order to proceed to the next higher level of success.

Let me wrap it up with this story. A young business man approached one of my seniors in the ecclesiastical service for help with his business. He complained to this elderly clergyman of how his business was not doing well. Some of the goods he bought to sell were almost getting old in his store and he wasn't getting the turnovers as he should.

The clergy gave him a very simple home assignment. He told him to go to his store, take a hard long look at all the items that have stayed long there, and begin to speak to them. He was to speak to the items to attract buyers. The man told him to start calling forth the buyers to come to his store and buy those items. That looked so simple but not so to the young trader. He asked, 'How can

I talk to things in my store? My neighbors would think that I am crazy.' The elderly man told him that was the solution if he wanted to sell those goods. So he left.

A month later, he came back with some gifts for the clergy. By then, this preacher couldn't recognize him. He introduced himself and narrated his story. He did exactly what the man had instructed him to do. As if the buyers were waiting for his invitation, and those goods were waiting for his orders, he was able to sell all of them. For the next weeks, he kept following that principle and things changed for the better for him. When you decide to adjust your beliefs and try certain principles that maybe strange to you, success might be your ultimate experience.

### Trying To Figure It Out

Curiosity is one basic trait of human beings. We want to always know the details and understand the workings before we try it. There's nothing wrong in being curious but we should not allow curiosity to hinder our chances of success. Curiosity can lead you to discovery of new ways and also blind you from discovering already available ways. It's like a two-edged sword; you must be careful how you handle it.

Whenever you want to figure out everything before you accept it as a way to achieve success, you may end up having a long way to get to success. The reason most people score high in school and low in life after school is that while in school they followed instructions, but after school they follow delusions. Check some of those people years after, they hardly figure out anything to make them succeed. Why? Because they abandon the real stuff that made successful people succeed while trying to figure out how those principles make people to succeed. No matter how intelligent or smart you are, you cannot really find out everything.

Success in life is mostly achieved by following what is making other people successful. It's more like copy and paste, and in some cases, copy, modify and paste. The wisest President Solomon said, *'The thing that has been — it is what will be again, and that which has been done is that which will be done again; and there is nothing new under the sun.'* What is going on in the world is recycling of former things. Moreover, no matter how you try, you cannot figure them out completely. So if you are someone who always employs sense in applying every principle, you will face this challenge, too.

In conclusion, the usefulness of your mouth is beyond eating, drinking, and talking. Your mouth has been given to you for your all-round well-being. How you use it to affect your life depends on the understanding you have. What this book has done is to show you what and how to actually achieve more than you have in terms of health, wealth, and a new life. You can recreate, reproduce, and reframe your life. With your mouth you can dismantle, destroy and disengage certain elements that are not complimentary to your life.

Your mouth is a solid weapon to wage war against forces that resist your growth. Such forces as poverty, sickness, retrogression, stagnation, doubts and fears can give way when you use your mouth in the right way to send them away. No one is going to speak for you when you are not speaking for yourself. When you shut your mouth you shut the door of your life. Good things won't come in and bad things won't leave. However, when you realize this truth and open your mouth, the things you do not want will obey your voice while the good things you desire will honor your invitation.

From this end, it is hoped that you will find this book helpful within the context it is shared. It is also my expectation that you will conquer whatever challenges you may face in accepting the issues raised in it. You are like me, but if you would take my advice, read this book again and again. Each reading time will present something fresh and new that will help you achieve the primary goal of the author — your all-round wellness. To appreciate it, recommend it to a friend or neighbor you love to buy a copy. I bet they will find it impacting. Do not forget: What your mouth cannot do does not exist. If they exist, it is because you have not used your mouth effectively.

<u>CONCLUSION</u>

Unleashing the Power Within you. Possible!

As we conclude this transformative journey into the realm of personal growth and empowerment, it is evident that our mouths are not merely instruments for communication but powerful weapons capable of waging war against the forces that resist our progress. Throughout the chapters, we have explored the intricate ways in which words shape our reality, influence our mindset, and ultimately determine the trajectory of our lives.

In the store of self-improvement, the spoken word appears as a solid weapon, a dynamic force capable of breaking down barriers, dispelling self-doubt, and forging a path toward unprecedented growth. The realization that our mouths hold such formidable power is both liberating and challenging. It underscores the responsibility we bear for the words we choose to wield, recognizing that each utterance carries the potential to build or destroy.

Our journey began with the understanding that self-awareness is the key to harnessing the potency of our words. By becoming mindful of the language we use, both in our internal dialogue and in external communication, we lay the foundation for a transformative process. Words are not only tools of expression but seeds planted in the fertile soil of our consciousness. Through conscious cultivation, we can nurture a garden of positive thoughts and affirmations that will blossom into the reality we desire.

The chapters that followed probed into the various dimensions of verbal warfare, unveiling strategies to overcome obstacles, face adversity, and silence the inner critic. We explored the art of constructive self-talk, recognizing its role as a compass guiding us toward our goals. Moreover, we discovered the profound impact of language on our relationships, as our words could either build bridges or erect walls between others and ourselves.

As we stand at the crossroads of our journey, it is essential to internalize the concept that our mouths are not only weapons against external challenges but also instruments of self-empowerment. By choosing words that affirm our assets, articulate our aspirations, and state our intentions, we take command of our destiny. The battles we face may be numerous and wide-ranging, but armed with the right words, we become builders of our own triumph.

In the striking embroidery of personal development, the conclusion is not a final chapter but a commencement—a launching pad into a future where the mastery of language continues to shape our evolution. As we navigate the complexities of life, let us remember that our mouths are not only capable of waging war against resistance but also of sowing the seeds of resilience, perseverance, and unyielding growth.

My prayer is that this exploration into the power of words serves as a perpetual reminder that, in the symphony of existence, our voices are instruments capable of composing a melody that resonates with the harmonies of success, fulfillment, and unbounded possibility. The journey to self-mastery is ongoing, and with each word we utter, we mold the masterpiece of our lives. Let the power within your mouth be the force that propels you to heights yet unseen, as you embrace the transformative journey that lies ahead. Let me leave you with these words of the wisest king who ever lived, *"'Words kill, words give life; they're either poison or fruit —you choose'* (Proverbs 18:21 TM).